CONTINUUM

CHELLA MAN

PENGUIN WORKSHOP

**For all who have come before me
and told their stories with pride.
By doing so, they cracked open the door.
I hope to take it off its hinges by continuing
their legacy with our communities.
—CM**

PENGUIN WORKSHOP
An Imprint of Penguin Random House LLC, New York

Penguin supports copyright. Copyright fuels creativity, encourages diverse voices, promotes free speech, and creates a vibrant culture. Thank you for buying an authorized edition of this book and for complying with copyright laws by not reproducing, scanning, or distributing any part of it in any form without permission. You are supporting writers and allowing Penguin to continue to publish books for every reader.

The publisher does not have any control over and does not assume any responsibility for author or third-party websites or their content.

Text copyright © 2021 by Chella Man. Illustrations on pages 6, 13, 21, 26, 29, 33, 37, 44, 49, 57, and 63 copyright © 2021 by Chella Man. All other illustrations copyright © 2021 by Penguin Random House LLC. All rights reserved. Published by Penguin Workshop, an imprint of Penguin Random House LLC, New York. PENGUIN and PENGUIN WORKSHOP are trademarks of Penguin Books Ltd, and the W colophon is a registered trademark of Penguin Random House LLC. Manufactured in China.

Visit us online at www.penguinrandomhouse.com.

Library of Congress Cataloging-in-Publication Data is available upon request.

ISBN 9780593223482   10 9 8 7 6 5 4 3 2 1

PROLOGUE

If I had been born during any other era, my story would be different. The world would not be ready to understand with open hearts or minds. To this day, many still choose not to. But whether they choose ignorance or empathy is up to them. My story will still be here; it will never be erased.

It begins and remains with a revelation: *All of who I am lies on a continuum.* My identity cannot be encompassed by a single term.

My ethnicity. I am biracial. I am both Jewish and Chinese.

My gender. I am genderqueer, existing outside the binary of "boy" and "girl."

My disability. I am Deaf with access to some sound

 5

through two cochlear implants.

My sexuality. I am pansexual, loving beyond "straight" or "gay."

I have not always known these identity expressions. To understand them, I first had to unlearn. It required diving deep into the systems that oppressed me, scraping the surface to expose them, and then studying their roots. And while it was terrifying, I understood that the communities standing by me would always offer support. That love and empathy (products of this ever-long process of discovery) can melt the cold, hard surface of the iceberg. Together, we will rebuild these systems around inclusivity and accessibility by embracing individuality and living our truths.

CONTINUUM

As soon as I could articulate my choices, I chose to paint my childhood bedroom blue. Looking back, it is clear that this decision was made in favor of the gender I wished to claim. Books and loose papers filled with doodles covered the floor—one thing that has never changed. From bed, I gazed up, scanning the edges of my ceiling, watching the blue meet the bare drywall. My body was engulfed by the tangled mess of superhero blankets as my pupils ran laps around the whites of my eyes, cycling through the routine in hopes it would shift my focus from the constant ringing in my ears. It was an eerie pitch, distant yet close, seeming to emanate from my mind.

At times, I wondered if the incessant noise was my own subconscious, passing on a message. Its voice kept me awake, encouraging my futile attempts of translation.

Enough, I thought, swinging my small legs over the side of the bed. I've never had much patience, although I have learned there are pros to this con. Letting my body drop the short distance from the bed to the ground, I walked down the hallway to my parents' bedroom.

Every year, my parents insisted on hanging my sister's and my school photos down this path. Passing them that night, I felt my own eyes follow me, bright from the moonlight. My mom always advised us to sport our favorite shirt each year on picture day. "Screw formality," she said. "When you look back, you'll connect with the clothing you loved."

Naturally, I chose to fill my frames with baggy Spider-Man T-shirts. Empowered to be in clothes I connected with, my smile was genuine. I wish this remained for the school pictures to come.

Reaching my parents' door, I cracked it open.

"Mommy?" I said, rubbing my eyes as they adjusted to the light.

"Rachel! Why are you awake? What's wrong?"

She rushed over and crouched down so we were eye to eye. My mom always tried to treat us as equals.

"My ears are ringing," I heard myself say.

A crease formed between her brows, and her shoulders softened.

"I thought the ringing would have stopped after a week, but I'll take you to the ear doctor tomorrow morning just to be safe, okay?"

"Okay."

I hugged her hard and retreated to my blue room.

The sky was an empty blue that morning as we sped down the highway toward the Hershey hospital. I watched the telephone poles pass, eyes darting back and forth, saturated fields of green blurring outside my window. We approached a huge billboard with bright blocks of colors and candy-themed cartoons smiling down at us. It read: *WELCOME TO HERSHEY: The Sweetest Place On Earth*. The scene epitomized Pennsylvania; nothing but cows, grass, and hollow sweetness.

"In and out," my mom assured me, knowing my lack of patience all too well. "It should be real quick!"

We anticipated a single appointment that day. But just when I thought we were finished, another was set up. The final appointment concluded with my audiologist entering the room, the smile on her face not quite reaching her eyes. She took her time to sit down across from us and cross her legs. When her eyes finally met my mom's, she waited a beat and said, "Your daughter seems to have a progressive hearing loss."

I shifted my eyes from hers to my mom's just in time to see the shock fill her face and her strength attempt to cover it. She listened silently as the audiologist continued, her hand reaching for mine, pulling it close, squeezing it tight.

The audiologist continued, "As of now, it is only a mild hearing loss, but there is no telling how much it will progress."

I did not understand the destiny these words cemented. My ability to hear would drift farther and farther away, placing me in a space between the hearing and the Deaf world. Nor did I foresee the side effects of prejudice and stigma would rise from both communities as a result. I did not anticipate the unlearning to come—how I would train my body to adapt; how language, as I knew it, had to expand for me to understand. I only felt concern for my mom, who was visibly shaken.

I also didn't realize that this unlearning had already begun. One year earlier, at three years old, I had shared two deep desires with my mom. The first was to shop in the boys' section of The Children's Place. The second was for my hair to be cut "short like the boys."

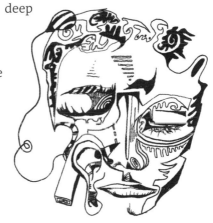

I always longed to walk into that store and turn left toward the boys' section, rather than right. While my mom was open to this decision and never stopped me from shopping there, her clothing preferences for me were clear. Whenever I leaned toward feminine clothes, she would comment on how beautiful I looked, my older sister chiming in with agreement. But when I gravitated toward clothes that were considered more masculine (such as brown and green dinosaur shirts), she would just smile in silence.

The haircut was another story. Though she was open to the masculine clothing, my mom denied this request. Lacking the language to articulate myself properly, I did what any child would do—I threw tantrums.

This phase continued for about two years, long enough for my mom to drag me to therapy. My actions and demands led her to worry that I was depressed. Of course, the therapist (a white, cisgender, nondisabled woman) took one look at me and had a perspective that mirrored the culture around her in central Pennsylvania. She lacked the education and experience to help me unpack what I was feeling as a disabled, queer child of color. We met a whopping total of two times before she concluded that I wasn't depressed. Apparently, I was handling the change in my hearing impressively well and not struggling in any way with my gender identity or orientation. "So there's really no need to continue," she told my mom.

Therapy was cut short, and my frustration continued to build. I learned that stubbornness, while often seen as a negative trait, saved me. I refused to give up who I knew I was, pleading for the haircut I longed for. Eventually, my mom grew tired of my tantrums, and we headed to a salon. *The war is won,* I thought. I was finally going to get the haircut that would bridge my body with my mind.

The familiar mixture of shampoo and hair dye wafted in the air as my mom and I entered the salon. Usually, those scents would trigger dread, but this time, they only amplified my excitement. Reaching the front desk, my mom and the haircutter spoke about my wishes. I could only pick up the words "pixie cut" being thrown around. *Really?* Even hairstyle names are gendered. To this day, the word "pixie" still makes me cringe. I hopped into the chair I had grown to hate, knowing this time would be different. Locking eyes with my reflection, I watched the shears dance around my head, gradually replacing disconnection with unity as my dark brown locks fell to the floor.

After this haircut, strangers *always* perceived me as a boy. Sometimes this made me feel closer to them than my own family. They saw *me*, not a constructed facade. That was until my mom would introduce me by clarifying, "This is my *daughter*, Rachel."

I always believed this was solely to frame my assigned gender to people. In her mind, she was trying to protect me from misgendering, though really, *she* was at fault for misgendering me. Recently, I learned this was only half the truth—her reaction was due to a separate stereotype, one of race.

"We did not look alike. As a white, Jewish woman, people in our small town did not realize I could be your mother. I introduced you this way to clarify that I was your mom."

Learning this repainted my memory. My mom was

also a victim of stereotypes. People often suspected we were adopted. That felt more believable than the potential of her being in a biracial relationship.

And it only made me wonder further: What other details had I missed?

One memory from childhood that I can't forget is my kindergarten circle time.

Rising from our doll-size desks, my classmates and I happily raced to the front of the class. I would always reach it first because I had the front-row seat, a requirement to better hear the teacher.

Watching all the kids plop down on the carpet after me, I found myself studying the various ways boys and girls carried themselves. "Femininity" seemed to be synonymous with gentle movements, shifting one's weight from one foot to the other. "Masculinity," on the other hand, required balanced weight to uphold a sturdy demeanor. I noticed my own inherent mannerisms fell into the latter.

In my school, I quickly became known as the boy named "Rachel." I became accustomed to shrugging these comments off, wearing my baggy dinosaur clothes with pride and carrying my body the way I felt most comfortable. I was happy. *This life is mine*, I thought. Even at that age, I knew it wasn't worth sacrificing myself for other people's comfort. Clearly, there were always two lessons during circle time: the ones led by the teacher and the ones I crafted myself.

Squeeeeal. My thoughts were interrupted by my freshly fitted hearing aids, squeaking as if they were releasing complaints bouncing around my head. I whipped my head around my kindergarten classroom to see if any of the other kids noticed. My classmates across from me were chattering playfully, oblivious to my glances. *Whew*, I breathed out, *I'm in the clear*.

But I thought too soon. I felt a sharp poke on my shoulder and turned to see the girl next to me smirk, then say loudly, "What *was* that? It hurt my ears!"

Sitting on the kindergarten carpet, I began to explain. "It's my hearing aid . . . Uhh, sometimes if I put my hands too close to my head, it makes that noise,"

I said, stumbling on my words. "Sorry!" Thus began the cycle of explaining and advocating for my identities. I wish I had known not to apologize for my disability. But in those moments, I prioritized acceptance over dignity.

"Whatever," she mumbled, scoffing and turning to face her friend sitting on the opposite side. I looked down at my sneakers, pressing my thumb into the Velcro, long and hard enough for it to leave a temporary mark. *I must be strong*, I told myself.

This was a pattern I'd come to know well. It exhausted me quickly while managing to also increase my frustrations. I was often met with the common response, "Never mind. Whatever. Never mind. Whatever. Never mind." It became an anthem for dismissal—one of the only songs I knew by heart. Each time it played, I found myself daydreaming of empathy. *If only others could experience my perspective, I doubt they would be so quick to dismiss me*, I thought to myself.

To process discrimination throughout the years, I've found solace by following two steps: first, acknowledging where this discrimination comes from, and second, persevering despite it. I acknowledge that discrimination often stems from ignorance. Although it stings to be misunderstood, others' ignorance does not *always* hold malicious intent. Focusing on this truth, I concentrate on healing myself in that moment through productive dissociation rather than painful projection. This awareness helps me decide my next action with reason rather than emotion.

Following this period of reflection, I persevere. This involves a choice: either I can advocate for myself and teach others how to avoid performing future discriminatory actions or I can walk away. To determine my response, I consider:

The situation (Will I have to work with these people again?)

My present emotions (Do I have enough energy to teach others right now?)

My relationships with those involved (Are these people I will see often?)

I often find myself choosing to advocate and teach. I hope that my labor is seen as an invitation for others to play a part in the growth of inclusivity and accessibility. Most often, this leads them to realize the range of existence beyond their own.

I've found that this process of acknowledgment and perseverance is a practice—one that I will always be refining. But most importantly, I have to ask myself the question: *What will heal me in this moment?* From creating art or writing in solitude to reaching out to my support system, the answer varies each time. Healing, too, lies on a continuum.

I'm going to let you in on a childhood secret: I used to be scared of burrito bars.

Fleeting interactions with strangers are bound to happen. These short encounters throughout my early years forced me to advocate for my Deafness even while I was still learning what that meant.

I'd wait in line, hands hanging at my sides, drumming on the boxy cargo pants I insisted on wearing in second grade. This external movement distracted me from my building anxiety. I'd move forward, slowly, fidgeting until I reached the front of the line. Drawing in a breath to steady my eyes on the employees' mouths, I'd channel my energy toward hearing and reading their lips. With every burrito question I could decipher, I felt as if I were in a video game and slowly leveling up. Base? Level up. Protein? Easy—level up. Toppings? Lettuce, pico de gallo, guacamole. Level up.

But, sometimes, I'd miss a question. Falling through the cracks like Mario, the game was cut short. I restarted by asking the employees to repeat the question. Oblivious to my Deafness, their annoyance burned through my skin in a glare. I felt like I could read their minds, a superpower I never wished for. *Why is this kid stumped by such simple questions?* Shame rose up my face in red. I just wanted a burrito, not to explain the validity of my disability.

Associating brief interactions with embarrassment, I began to avoid food lines and cashiers. If possible, I would ask a friend to order for me, then pay them back. Sacrificing my autonomy for this solution, I promised myself it was only temporary.

As I grew, I practiced phrases in the bathroom mirror. "I am Deaf," I said. "If you could look at me when speaking, it would help me read your lips, or you could write it down, thank you." Or "I don't want you to think I am ignoring you, so I want to let you know I am Deaf!" I even used "Sorry, I am deaf. Can you repeat that again, please?" But I have since learned to never apologize for my disability.

Overall, I believed these clarifications would halt ableism. In some cases, it did! In others, not so much. Far too often, employees would cock their heads in doubt. Perplexed by the reaction, I unconsciously mirrored their movements in confusion. Then, it dawned on me: *They think I'm lying.* Stereotypically, key indicators of an individual being Deaf are having a deaf accent or using sign language. I did not have a deaf accent and had only recently begun ASL (American Sign Language) lessons in third grade. English was my first language, so I typically did not use sign language.

So, there I was, advocating for my disability, hoping it would clarify my needs and enable employees to better support me. But somehow, I was deemed "not-deaf-enough" by hearing people. *There must be something wrong with me*, I would think.

I later realized that the employees' perspectives erased the variations an identity can encompass. They saw deafness as one thing, relying on stereotypes to distinguish millions of people in the Deaf community. In fact, my decision to identify as capital "D" Deaf has been recent. Growing up without other Deaf individuals surrounding me, I was not connected to Deaf culture. Today, my Deaf identity represents a huge part of who I am, how I navigate this world, and I am surrounded by my own Deaf, chosen family. The truth is, identity isn't a monolith. It exists on a continuum, reflecting our own specific experiences and personhood.

Even in Deaf spaces, I've still been categorized as an outsider. When I was eleven, I attended a summer sleepaway camp at a Deaf school in Pennsylvania. Leaving home for the first time alone was daunting, but I believed the Deaf community would accept me in a way that the hearing community never had.

Reaching the school after a few hours of driving, I cautiously exited the car. The world was silent but full of movement. Kids and adults swarmed the campus, hands flying. There were so many conversations existing in silence. After signing in, the parents departed, leaving all of us to start the camp icebreakers.

The camp had us all break off into smaller groups to connect. I watched all the other kids sign with fluency, intimidated to say the least. Facing one another in a small circle, a counselor began the domino of introductions. By the time it was my turn, I was exhausted. As I raised my hands slowly to communicate, the other kids instantly realized my lack of fluency.

When the icebreakers concluded, everyone broke off and began to form groups of their choosing. No one spoke to me; they did not want to deal with the language barrier. I was isolated in the one space I had hoped would prove accessible to me. Despite it all, adults attempted to console me with the mantra "Just be yourself." Little did they know, that was exactly what I was trying to do.

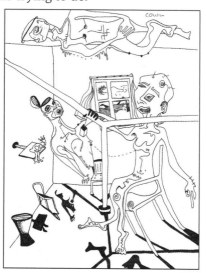

Reflecting on the challenges of simultaneously navigating my disability and queerness in conservative Pennsylvania, I've noticed a stark contrast between the two identities: My disability was interpreted as a medical issue, producing conversation and resources. But when it came to my gender and sexuality, the world went dark.

My parents are both medical professionals, which allowed them to comfortably engage within the disability dialogue. Holding these conversations supplied me with tools to understand my disability on a deeper level. Appointments with my audiologists, speech therapists, and Deaf educators required me to understand the anatomy of the ear and medical terms like "sensorineural." Queerness seemed to exist beyond this universe. My parents had no personal experience or understanding of queer culture outside of the general stereotypes and stigmas. Simply believing I was "going through a tomboy phase," they were lost. I was able to locate the discrimination I faced due to my disability. But I had no perspective of anti-queer prejudice to help me navigate my gender and sexuality.

By the time I was in fourth grade, deaf discrimination wasn't the only kind I was exposed to.

My gender was being scrutinized every day, at every moment. I had been confronted countless times in the girls' bathroom, analyzed by adults trying to figure out my genitalia, forced to strip and change clothes in a locker room with my "female" classmates.

I distinctly remember one morning when a new boy boarded the school bus, clearly doing his best to put on a strong face. His name was Tyler. I noticed other kids avoiding his gaze as he searched for an open seat. So when he reached me, I met his eyes and slid closer to the window. He nodded silently with gratitude and quickly sat down, releasing the breath he had been holding.

We immediately became friends, always meeting up at recess to kick a ball around.

One afternoon, Tyler invited a few boys to play with us. "Do you want to play with me and him?"

A second of excruciating silence passed before . . . "Dude, that's a girl!"

Tyler whipped his head around, brow furrowed

and eyes searching. I felt naked from this remark, humiliated as Tyler began scrutinizing me. Reading the shame on my face, his expression went slack. This was all he needed to confirm their accusation. He sat somewhere else on the bus the next morning.

With fifth grade fast approaching, puberty began to chip away the pieces of my body I connected to the most. Gender dysphoria[1] blossomed in their place. My chest and curves became accentuated, peeking out of the shadows of "passing." It became impossible to hide any longer from feminine gender roles. Shame and fear led me to regress toward the lessons I had learned in circle time. My desire to be authentic suddenly blurred under the pressures of adhering to the gender binary.

1. Gender dysphoria is when a person experiences extreme discomfort or distress because they do not connect with their physical body.

I began to rewire. For hours, I would study myself in the mirror, molding my mannerisms to be her. *Remember to shift your weight to one foot and let your arms fall loosely down*, I would whisper to myself, discarding the balanced and sturdy movements that came naturally to me. *This will make you look gentle.*

Next, I focused on clothing. To test the waters, I approached my older sister, Maya. As I passed the hallway lined with my old school photos, the boy named Rachel watched me take the steps to erase him. Reaching Maya's bedroom, I cracked open the door.

"Maya . . . ? Can you help me with something?"

She looked at me quizzically, then said, "Sure! What is it?"

"I want to wear your clothes tomorrow."

Her eyes widened in disbelief, then flickered with excitement—a familiar reaction. Jumping up from her bed, she began to leaf through her closet. Hunkering down behind her, I drew in a silent breath. *There's no turning back now*, I thought. *This is what you are supposed to find FUN. Learn to enjoy it . . .*

"Here! This is perfect!" Maya exclaimed gleefully, interrupting my silent pep talk.

I gazed up at a tight, gray Aéropostale shirt paired with a fake pearl necklace. It was the pinnacle of fourth-grade fashion, and I was going for it.

As I stepped onto the school bus the next day, the neighborhood kids nudged one another in silent shock. In an instant, however, the reaction morphed into encouragement through comments on my feminine beauty. I even remember multiple kids exclaiming, "Look! Rachel *is* a girl!"

The underlying relief from these reactions confirmed what I'd always suspected: These responses, while positive, promoted the erasure of individuality. Before, my identity was uncategorizable, leaving others uncomfortable, as we are taught to fear the unknown. The longer I stayed true to myself, the more this fear built inside others. I had to give up my authentic self to survive.

Thinking on it now, having a queer role model to aspire toward could have saved parts of me I've since had to recover. Perhaps their visibility would've coaxed me to share my desire to live as I felt inside. Or perhaps I would've simply acknowledged their existence from afar, noting that an honest life past binaries was possible. Perhaps that would've been enough.

By middle school, I became "Rachel" in all her glory. I had lost all my friends who were boys, so I scrambled to form a secure friend group among the girls. My hair had lengthened to my shoulders. Every morning, I burned it against its natural curves. Sizzling beneath the straightener heat, I cemented it to fit conventional beauty standards.

I continued to wear clothes I otherwise never would've been drawn to. I practiced feminine mannerisms, believing that repetition could reprogram my inherent behavior. I waited for this to come true. But each day, every mirror reflected a lie. I was miserable inside. I mourned for my true identity and my body before puberty.

Close friends and family began to laugh and smile

when recalling my "tomboy" phase, as if my identity then had been a joke. To cover my own pain with connection, I would join them. For seven years, this performance continued. Of course, I never forgot about him—the one I knew I truly was at my core.

Sophomore year of high school was the first time I was asked out. A cute boy I had been crushing on asked me to the movies, and it caught me off guard. I had never received attention from my crushes before. Like many trans and disabled kids, my self-confidence had been impinged by gender dysphoria, transphobia, and ableism. I did not believe anyone could truly see me as beautiful.

I said yes right away, even though the plan was to see a movie—a simple event for nondisabled individuals yet complex for me. Though hearing aids and cochlear implants increased my ability to hear, I still struggle to piece together verbal communication. Most theaters refuse to have open captioning because hearing individuals complain that the open captions are "annoying and distracting." To avoid disrupting the experiences of these nondisabled individuals, bulky devices called CaptiViews (external captioning systems) are available. The problem is that they usually don't work, are rarely cleaned, and are primarily used by theaters to create the illusion of inclusion rather than supporting true accessibility through providing open captioning.

(Also, can I just say, even for hearing people, seeing a movie is a terrible first date. You sit in complete darkness, unable to talk for the majority of the time. I took my girlfriend to the park on our first date, which was well lit and quiet, perfectly accessible to me, and we talked for three-plus hours. Anyway, back to the story.)

On the day of the date, our moms had to drop us off. Classic. Sitting next to my crush in the dark movie theater without captions, I pretended to follow and enjoy the story projected. To this day, I have no idea what that movie was about.

I wish I had not compromised my accessibility and enjoyment in this situation. The stigma of disability left me fearful of holding open conversations, especially within new relationships. I realize now—it is not my *disability* that is uncomfortable. It is others' *obliviousness* about navigating and supporting those with a disability that created the conflict.

The obstacle could have been easily overcome if I had told him, "Hey, I would absolutely love to go to the movies with you. As you know, I'm Deaf, so I typically need captions on the screen to follow along. Could we see a foreign movie that has subtitles, or watch Netflix at one of our houses instead?" Either option would have created a much better date. If standing up for myself turned him away, I would have known he lacked empathy and understanding. I wouldn't have wanted to be with him anyway.

That is one of the beauties of my identity. It acts as a filter, guiding me toward the gems in life.

Throughout the next year, I began to explore cultures and communities through social media. Even though I was still stuck in central Pennsylvania, physical boundaries melted away online. I virtually diversified my life by filling my timelines with queer, disabled, and/or people of color who spoke honestly about their lives. My own inability to categorize the others I followed affirmed my belief that no actual boundaries existed. Their stories reflected human experiences, which is to say everything and nothing at all.

All of a sudden, I had watched gay men kiss in

public, lesbians hold each other and laugh, Asian and Jewish individuals speak openly about living in America, and even Deaf artists sharing their truth. Although I had not yet discovered identities past binaries, I had more hope than before.

Most of these connections were one-sided. I quietly followed and read the perspectives of others. Instead of directly speaking to them, as one would in person, I held conversations with myself, ignited by their words. The relationship that developed there united me with my community as well as my own identity. I finally had a front-row seat to the dialogue happening within my own cultures.

I began to feel connected. The parts of myself I kept hidden began to claw at the layers of repression that had cemented. Refusing to repress my queerness any longer, I stayed up one night, scrolling through endless definitions inside queer dictionaries, trying to find the perfect words to encompass my gender and sexuality.

By dawn, I held two words in my mind. Pacing back and forth in the morning light, with my adrenaline pumping, my fear mixed with euphoria. I suddenly stopped and spotted my notebook in the corner. Clutching the lined paper, I allowed the walls within me to collapse. I wrote: *I am pansexual: open to all and any genders; and I am gender-fluid: not having a fixed gender.*

Not only had these words affirmed the gender and sexual identities I always felt, but I knew there must be entire communities behind each term. I was not alone.

Now, I dislike the term "coming out" because it should not be a necessary event. But that is what happened the next morning with my family. I was terrified, but I had the huge privilege of knowing they would accept me and adjust with time. To share my epiphany with the rest of the world, I wrote a post on Instagram, introducing my new identities accompanied by their definitions. I smiled to myself with a lightness I had not felt in years. The relief and liberation I felt that day . . . whew. Words cannot describe.

I must say, these terms are not far from how I would describe myself today—so good job, baby queer Chella! To this day, I still identify my sexuality as pansexual, but refrain from using gender-fluid. Since educating myself deeper on queer terminology, my identity has evolved. I now use the term "genderqueer." For me, this translates as not subscribing to the gender binary but, rather, existing outside it.

"Donald Trump is coming to speak at our school," announced the animated voice of my principal one morning over the loudspeaker. I couldn't believe my ears. I didn't want to believe my ears. I hoped, for the first time, that I had misheard the information.

As I sat in my junior-year homeroom, my head spun, attempting to process this. *Donald Trump is coming to speak at our school.* The bell rang promptly after this announcement, and I watched kids I grew up with explode into the hallway with joy. Their cheers bounced off the hallway lockers. *This cannot get any worse*, I thought as I saw my classmates celebrate a man who encourages hate and violence toward individuals like me. But then, a cry rang out, stopping me in my tracks and proving me wrong. "Electrocute the gays!" Laughter erupted. I knew, then, I could not stand another year there.

This news magnified the numbness I already felt in my hometown. For years, I cycled through the daily routine of going to school, heading straight home to sleep until 3:00 a.m., finishing my homework, creating art (if time permitted), and repeating. I felt like a machine, and my fuel was my dream of leaving Pennsylvania.

Thankfully, I've always had an openhearted relationship with my mom, and I was clear about what I wanted even before this announcement: I dreamed of moving to New York City. She began to research academic programs in NYC for juniors in high school. And on one glorious day, she stumbled upon Parsons School of Design's early-acceptance program. The application closed within a week. Frantically, she grabbed her phone and texted me: *I think I found a way for you to get out of Pennsylvania. FaceTime me.*

Skip senior year and move directly to New York City for college? *Are you kidding me? This is nothing short of a dream.*

The application called for solid grades and an art portfolio. With the deadline only a week away, the next seven days were a frenzy. Not only was I applying for college early, but it was also the final-exam week for my current semester. If I did not get into college then, my grades for the exams were still crucial. Stress was high. Hopes were higher.

A few weeks later, the Parsons' admissions director requested a video call. I told my family to wait downstairs as I set up my laptop and called New York City from my childhood bedroom. I nervously waited for the line to connect, a moment that's now locked in my brain forever. Looking around the blue walls of my bedroom, I let my eyes rest and fall into the color.

Ding ding ding!

The line connected, pulling me back to the present. The director of admissions had a smile on her face. My eyes widened as she began to speak. She informed me that I was the only junior who was accepted and that she was also offering me a scholarship.

I thanked her numerous times before signing off. Had the chat been in person, I would have jumped out of my seat and given her a ginormous hug! Grinning from cochlear implant to cochlear implant, I opened the door to race downstairs and share the news with my family. Turns out my mom had her ear pressed to the door outside. She was crying tears of joy.

My dad congratulated me. My sister, already away for college, cheered with me over FaceTime.

For the first time in a while, I felt that cycle of numbness shatter. *This is it*, I thought. *I am getting out.*

Leaving my blue room behind, I began a new chapter in New York City. Immediately, I experienced culture shock. I felt as if I had been living under a rock in central Pennsylvania. At long last, the diverse culture I had observed on social media became tangible.

In New York City, queer culture surrounded me. Trans individuals were not mythical but real people I could befriend. There were art events for the Deaf community (like ASL Slam), and people of varying ethnicities zoomed through the streets.

As I settled into this new culture and college life, conversations of diversity, accessibility, and inclusivity were being held inside and outside the classrooms. Many of the individuals now surrounding me were also part of a minority community, meaning these topics impacted them deeply, too. Eager to explore our own histories and systems, I was able to hold fervent conversations with a newfound level of interconnection. These moments affirmed many of my own experiences with bigotry growing up, encouraging me to further understand my identities.

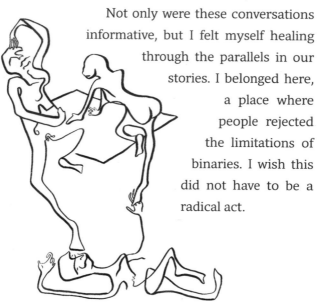

Not only were these conversations informative, but I felt myself healing through the parallels in our stories. I belonged here, a place where people rejected the limitations of binaries. I wish this did not have to be a radical act.

With my growing sense of self, I was eager to further explore my new atmosphere. And so on the night of September 16, 2016, my new friends and I found out about a house party happening in Bushwick, Brooklyn—the kind you can smell from a block away because of the kids smoking out of the upstairs window. All the first years seemed to be planning on letting loose that night.

This is where I met her. She arrived before me, with friends at the start of the party. Once they got through the doors, her group dispersed. Alone, she wandered through the house. An hour later, I arrived with my friends, and we ended up in the same room.

Spotting me from across the room, she recalled seeing me once before in our school café from a distance, my bald head with "something behind my ears" catching her eye. At the time, I used she/her pronouns and appeared femme. Studying me again from a distance, she decided to approach me.

Gently weaving through the smoke and huddled college kids, she moved toward me. The first words she said to me were "Hey, I like your hair."

I don't have any, I thought, chuckling to myself. Smiling down at her, I remember thinking, *She seems like the coolest person in the room.* I replied, "Thanks, what's your name?"

"MaryV."

This was the first time I'd heard her name; I'd never met anyone with it before.

"Ah, I'm Chella."

We ended up talking for a few minutes. Not long, but enough for my heart to quicken as I took in her beauty. Light freckles kissed her face and lips, framed with dark red hair and amber eyes to match. The few minutes passed, and we were split up by the commotion of the party as it raged on.

I didn't see her until hours later. Most kids had left by then. I wondered if she had, too. But then I saw her in the same room we were in before. Leaning against the brick wall, her focus rested on her friend, who was passed out on the bed. She was making sure he was safe. This is something I know well now: her tendency to become a guardian angel to those she loves.

Two people next to him were deep in a make-out

session. MaryV found humor in the intensity and raised her phone to snap a photo to remember. I made my way to her as she looked up from her phone. She smiled at me as I approached her. Reunited again, we leaned against the wall and laughed together at the cliché college situation in front of us.

Then, there was a pause in conversation. I looked at her, knowing I would regret leaving the party without asking her out. I hesitated for a moment, acknowledging her "feminine" appearance. If I acted based off of stereotypes, I would guess her sexuality to be straight—a completely idiotic thing to conclude based on looks alone.

So, I launched the question: "This is really random, but would you want to go out sometime?"

It hung in the air, and I could tell that MaryV's thoughts were racing. I know now that she was thinking, *Is this a date? No, this cool girl definitely just wants to be friends and hang out.*

After a hesitation that felt like forever, she answered, "Yeah, sure, let's hang out! Put your number in my phone."

At the time, the rose emoji was MaryV's thing. She added it to her contact name and texted herself one to have my number in her phone. MaryV's contact remains unchanged today. After the exchange, MaryV asked me to show her the bathroom. My friends were leaving then, so I had to head out without saying goodbye. Instead, I sent her a rose back.

I had no idea MaryV actually considered herself to be straight at the time—a fact she told me on our first date, which she didn't actually know was a date. Even after I learned this, we continued to hang out. During this time, she allowed herself to think more about her sexuality, which was quite a good thing for me because, lo and behold, she turned out to not be straight.

whew

Four years later, I'm still thankful she complimented my nonexistent hair that night. MaryV has taught me to love myself as much as I love her. I cannot count how many times she has grounded me by holding on and reminding me to take a breath. She has learned to listen to my hands, erasing the communication barrier between us. When we flick off the lights and climb into bed at night, my implants are off.

I see nothing.
I hear nothing.
MaryV wraps
her arms around
me while my hand
finds hers. I feel
her fingers twist
into a sign.
Pinkie up.
Middle and ring
down. Index up.
Thumb out.
It's how we say,
"I love you,"
in the dark.

I don't believe
in fate or soulmates,
but I do believe in
luck. And I got so
damn lucky with her.

MY LOVE & I

As I fell in love with MaryV and the new universe around me, I continued to learn from the stories and people in my life. I found myself particularly drawn to the experiences of my trans friends. Their life stories and connections to their bodies felt . . . relatable. It was something I had always known but never had the language and community support to help me articulate. Throughout my first year in New York City, I began to identify the intense, lingering feeling of discomfort as gender dysphoria. With this new terminology in hand, I began to search for ways to alleviate it.

As winter turned into spring, the possibilities began to blossom in my mind. As buds morphed into petals, I grew more confident of my desires, and one morning, I could not hold it in any longer. The moment felt as emotional as the day I "came out" in high school.

I needed to be with my thoughts. I needed to figure out what this meant. I needed to walk. I left my dorm room and my cochlear implants behind, heading into the New York City rush with a notebook and a new sense of urgency.

Can you imagine moving through the loudest city in the world in complete silence? Every other sense is heightened, but the city's mayhem is created through its energy and vibrations. Passing each block, I slowly became conscious of the way I avoided my own reflection in the city's windows. To glance over would mean perceiving my body from the side, a perspective that would only accentuate a body that was not mine.

What I wanted was undeniable; it always had been. I sat down on the sidewalk and pulled out my notebook. I stared at my pen, knowing the ink was permanent, just as the words would be. *Breathe*, I commanded myself. *Now, write.*

I gazed down at the words cemented onto the paper before me: *I want top surgery.*

To clarify, the goal was never to transition into a "man." As a genderqueer individual, I viewed my body without labeling the parts as a specific gender. I just wanted a flat chest. I was not even sure if I wanted to take testosterone, though a common misconception is that top surgery and testosterone must go hand in hand. *Perhaps the flat chest would be enough for my mind and body to feel more connected*, I thought. I feared testosterone would diminish my "feminine" qualities such as compassion, sensitivity, or empathy. Such a thought is unsurprising after being taught these qualities are only acceptable within femininity. To move past this fear, I had to unlearn and reframe where my characteristics originated. These attributes are part of who I am, regardless of my gender identity. Dismantling this myth enabled me to reconsider starting testosterone.

Yet there was still one stereotype blocking me. Questions zoomed around my head. Would I have to identify as a binary man once I started to look more masculine? And if I presented stereotypically masculine, would I have to let go of my genderqueer identity?

Luckily, I had an older close friend who was on testosterone and identified as nonbinary. Their very existence was added proof of gender existing past the binary. I realized that the way I presented myself did not have to fit any stereotype of the gender identity I claimed. This understanding was freeing. I would not have to sacrifice any part of myself to move forward. So I began to consider taking testosterone injections. I had no idea what I would end up looking like, but I hoped to gain more muscle mass, facial hair, and an overall "masculine" look.

Having a more solidified sense of self, I felt prepared to share my want for top surgery with the ones I loved. Each conversation I had was documented with a Polaroid photo. The first person I told was MaryV.

"What are you thinking about?" she asked me, as we lay in silence together on her dorm bed. There was a long pause. My heartbeat quickened, and my vision dashed around the room with each pulse. Between my hesitation and her question, I checked in with myself. *I feel safe, I'm going to tell her.*

"I've been thinking . . . I want top surgery." The moment I said it, I felt more naked than the first time we had sex. I studied her face, waiting for a reaction. She looked back at me, eyes steadily locked on mine. And I realized, for the first time, that someone had truly seen me and knew everything. No wonder I felt naked.

I continued. "I know I definitely want a flat chest, but am still figuring out if I want to start testosterone too. Right now, I don't. But, that may change later as I consider it further."

Eyes still locked, she was giving me her full attention. I felt love from her gaze.

"I also want to be transparent with you. Throughout this process, I am going to have to be selfish at times. This transitional phase will be filled with heavy emotions and healing. I want you to know, none of this is your responsibility to deal with. I love you, and I want you to stay. But, I also know this is an unfair expectation. So . . . I want to give you an out."

I paused. "You don't have to give me an answer right this second. You can leave if you want to, and I will be okay."

I stopped. She processed. After a few moments, she finally said, "I'm proud of you for telling me this. I support you one hundred percent." She did not consider the "out" I offered her for one second. In her mind, it was not an option. She later took a photo of me that night, lying on her dorm bed in the same position we held the conversation in with my chest exposed.

Over the next week, I told Maya over FaceTime, and separately had a conversation with my parents in person. I have all these moments documented through video recordings, and the one question I kept getting asked by MaryV, Maya, and my parents was "Are you sure?" Now they all understand the pain this unnecessary question can bring. Of course, if I was sharing this with them, I was sure. I had been sure my entire life. I have always known who I am.

In the end, their responses were filled with love. All of them offered their support. As doctors, my parents' main worry was how safe it would be to medically transition. To have this type of support is a huge privilege, although it should be the common response. I am grateful, every day, to have a family that has accepted my genderqueer identity and desire to medically transition. I will always strive for a world in which this is no longer rare.

To begin the process was itself a process. To receive top surgery and start testosterone, I had to acquire a letter from a licensed therapist (no knowledge of trans experience was necessary) to diagnose me with gender dysphoria. I also learned some insurances would not cover top-surgery costs unless the patient had been on hormones for at least one year. I remember wondering why cisgender therapists and economic professionals with no knowledge of trans experience had the power of gatekeeping the choice I made about my *own* body. Choosing to medically transition is a personal decision that should be accessible to all. Unfortunately, it is unavailable to many and remains a huge privilege. It's also important to note that those who do not wish to medically transition are just as valid as anyone else.

As the date of my first testosterone shot approached, I reflected on the boy named Rachel. I realized how far I had come. Communities within

New York City had empowered me enough to take the steps to reach this point. Yet, part of me still craved a community that would fully mirror all my identities. I had hoped New York City would gift me this, but I was still searching for those who matched my Deaf, genderqueer, 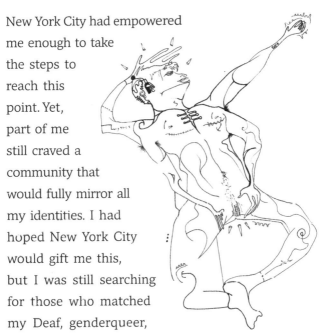 Chinese, Jewish, and transmasculine identities.

Finally, I realized the power of my own agency. New York City could not grant me that matching connection, but its communities lit my path to affirmation. I no longer had to wait for someone else to have my every identity. I decided to be my own representation.

On June 29, 2017, I gave myself the first testosterone shot with the guidance of my mom, while MaryV documented the milestone on her 35mm camera in front of a white backdrop. Sharing these images with personal writings on social media, I hoped the transparency of my experiences would serve as an educational resource. Following this, I continued to publicly document my life—highlighting the process of taking testosterone and getting top surgery, navigating the world as a Deaf individual, and sharing my love as I fell deeper with MaryV. She, too, documented her perspectives through videos, writing, performance pieces, and images. I wanted to show people how my identity (and my communities) transcended tokenization or stereotype. My core value was to keep the content as accessible as possible; I knew how life-changing accessible knowledge could be. Exposing such intimate experiences to the public had its challenges, but the representation it served was my top priority. It was a revolution within myself, and the result was an unexpected outpouring of love from my community.

To this day, I'm stunned and overwhelmed by the support. I've had the opportunity to connect with many others who are also living on the continuum. From speaking at colleges, sharing art, and holding meetups around the world, my greatest honor has been the feedback some of you have shared with me, letting MaryV and me know our content has been helpful in some way in your lives. I have found my representation not only within myself but within all of you.

Returning home from college after my first year in New York City, I sneaked into my sister's room to read her diary. (Definitely not my proudest moment, and I have since apologized to my sister—sorry again, Maya!) It was spring break, and she wasn't home. Flipping hungrily through the pages, I believed the secrets of adulthood would be revealed. Though my sister was only twenty, and I was seventeen, this span of three years seemed light-years apart. As I skimmed the pages flipping before me, my birth name caught my eye. The use of my old name instantly told me it was an old entry. I peered at the page, eager to know the words I was never supposed to read.

I feel sad today. Rachel told me she doesn't believe anyone would ever want her or fall in love with her. It would be too much work.

I never knew words could knock the wind out of you. It was as if someone had taken a stack of my old memories off a dusty shelf and presented them to me. I knew I was supposed to live the entirety of my life without ever seeing those words. But I was thankful my sister had recorded them, since I had not been in a space where I could do so myself. Cautiously, I turned inward to analyze my rising emotions. I expected to find open wounds, but surprisingly, I stumbled upon overwhelming relief.

Sitting with my old beliefs, I was reminded of all the experiences that led me here—from Hershey to New York City, from unlearning to learning, from Rachel to Chella, from acknowledgment to perseverance. I realized I had been wrong. My life held passionate relationships with love of all kinds.

The communities I met online and off have become a second family, one I chose. MaryV and I only grow deeper in love as we approach four years together. And I've grown closer with my mom, dad, and sister since opening up to them more. In fact, in a recent conversation with my mom, we reflected on the haircut moment from my childhood.

"For the boy haircut, I did not want to deny you the look you wanted. My initial hesitation was fear of how others would 'misgender' you," she said. "I thought that might bother you and potentially lead to teasing. I also remember restaurant servers would assume you were a boy, so I would clearly announce you were my daughter. I thought I was protecting you. Sadly, I realize how ironic this is now, of course."

She continued, "Once, I even asked you how you felt about being perceived as a boy. You said you liked it. I was shocked. Why that did not make me ask you more about that, I cannot explain. Honestly, it mystifies me how clueless and uninformed I was."

Her self-reflections and apologies have allowed

our relationship to heal and blossom. She has learned to hold herself accountable because accountability is an act of love.

Now, at twenty-one years old, I have learned to find empowerment within my identities. I'm allowing myself to believe in the love I receive as well as the love I deserve—the love that is possible to hold for myself.

Above all, I've learned that I am continuously learning. I definitely do not have it all figured out. I doubt I ever will, and I am learning to be okay with that. We are all running on different frequencies and discovering ourselves at different moments.

This continuum, this process of endless discovery, is why I've found it nearly impossible to create an ending to this book. Endings hold closure, but my story is far from over.

ABOUT US

Pocket Change Collective was born out of a need for space. Space to think. Space to connect. Space to be yourself. And this is your invitation to join us.

These books are small, but they are mighty. They ask big questions and propose even bigger solutions. They show us that no matter where we come from or where we're going, we can all take part in changing the communities around us. Because the possibilities of how we can use our space for good are endless.

So thank you. Thank you for picking this book up. Thank you for reading. Thank you for being a part of the Pocket Change Collective.